"Know Your True Worth"

Beyond MAN'S Expectations

"Know Your True Worth"

SERVANT DR. JERRY JOHNSON SR.

XULON PRESS

Xulon Press
2301 Lucien Way #415
Maitland, FL 32751
407.339.4217
www.xulonpress.com

© 2021 by Servant Dr. Jerry Johnson Sr.

All rights reserved solely by the author. The author guarantees all contents are original and do not infringe upon the legal rights of any other person or work. No part of this book may be reproduced in any form without the permission of the author. The views expressed in this book are not necessarily those of the publisher.

Due to the changing nature of the Internet, if there are any web addresses, links, or URLs included in this manuscript, these may have been altered and may no longer be accessible. The views and opinions shared in this book belong solely to the author and do not necessarily reflect those of the publisher. The publisher therefore disclaims responsibility for the views or opinions expressed within the work.

Unless otherwise indicated, Scripture quotations taken from the New American Standard Bible (NASB). Copyright © 1960, 1962, 1963, 1968, 1971, 1972, 1973, 1975, 1977, 1995 by The Lockman Foundation. Used by permission. All rights reserved.

Paperback ISBN-13: 978-1-66281-665-9
Ebook ISBN-13: 978-1-66281-666-6

TABLE OF CONTENTS

Chapter 1: Inferior to None 1

Chapter 2: Gender Equality 5

Chapter 3: A Wife Is That Good Thing 9

Chapter 4: Don't Think Like Man 11

Chapter 5 Likewise, Surrender and
            Honor Thy Husband 13

Chapter 6: Wife Deceitful Charter & Work 17

Chapter 7: A Woman Who Fears the Lord 21

Chapter 8: The Challenge Response:
            Women Know Your Worth 25

INTRODUCTION

Women, you may not have fared well in the world's religions, but you are greatly loved by God who, in the beginning, created women equal to men. The discrimination that women go through does not come from the heart of God. He created both men and women in His own image, with a capacity to know Him in a personal relationship. And when sin destroyed that relationship, God redeemed women through the death of His own Son. And one day, He will welcome into His heavenly home every woman who has claimed Jesus Christ as her personal Savior and Lord: and the equality, respect, and status she has longed for will be her's forever.

This book extends to readers the beauty and love of a godly woman, which encourages them to become that type of woman. It also discusses what their true relationship would look like with God and their husbands if they were free of "man's expectations," allowing them to develop their own expectations from God's point of view to truly know their value and realize it in life.

This book will be particularly engaging for female readers. While the book's primary role remains to be a core text for women, it will also encourage men to look at the expectations they place on women. Packed with biblical teaching applications readers will find particularly useful, *Beyond Man's Expectations: Know Your True Worth* is the first book of the "Beyond Series," which offers applied views of subjects via the inclusion of servant Dr. Jerry Johnson Sr.'s insights.

Within this powerful book of spiritual teaching, women will learn how to exceed the expectations of man and live the lives that God has intended for them based on His Word. With biblical insight, Christ-centered wisdom, and inspiration for everyday living, the author motivates women to seek God's plan for their lives.

Each section of the book contains biblical wisdom and real-life application, inspiring readers to embrace truth directly from God's Word while educating them with practical teaching that will help them apply the truths in their own lives. This balance brings God's Word to life in both practical and spiritual ways, motivating readers to dive deeper into the lifestyle God has destined for women.

Throughout the book, readers will see various teaching methods, such as biblical teaching, practical examples for readers, and experiences to which they can relate. These elements of the book's teachings provide a well-rounded understanding of how to see beyond the expectations of a man and live the life of a woman after God's heart.

Overall, women will be inspired by the possibilities of living a life of purpose and fulfillment that is pleasing to God.

First, though, let's look at what happens if a woman looks beyond man's expectations. Women live in a world where men often expect them to act and be a certain way, depending on the relationship they share, whether personal or professional. All women have to face these kinds of expectations to some degree.

Yes, women—you will be faced with expectations from men throughout life, and those expectations can be high or low, reasonable or unreasonable, good or bad. They can often create stress and anxiety that end up causing you as a woman to act in a way that turns the expectation into a reality.

- For example, when a man and woman get married, the man's expectations may be that his wife must be caring, kind, a good cook, and patient. He forms expectations about what she will be like as a mother. If she does not turn out to be a patient wife or a particularly good cook, he may feel hurt and let down, and can end up resenting her because of what he had *hoped* would happen. You made no promises, but he still feels as though he has been deceived.

Many times, those expectations will have you unable to find solace, happiness, or satisfaction. You must learn to take a step toward God and His Word to ensure you are pursuing and preserving your own expectations, happiness, and health. So, as you began to focus more on your own expectations, you will begin to drift away from thoughts built on the foundation of what man expects.

Let the women say there is hope in God's Word. The Bible encourages those who trust in the Lord to expect good things from Him. "My soul, wait thou only upon God; for my expectation is from him" (Ps. 62:5).

Here are three values that the Bible presents to help women look beyond man's expectations:

Communicate: Communicating with sincerity and truthfulness with yourselves and man is the first key. We all fail ourselves and others in many ways (Jas. 3:2), and you should be able to admit when you are wrong. You should not base your expectations on mere assumption but on verifiable truth. You should discuss with men what yours and their expectations are.

Forgive: The people in Jesus's day were expecting the Messiah (Lk. 3:15), but when He came, they had some unrealistic expectations of what He'd do. They wanted the Messiah to free them from Rome, and they wrongly expected Jesus to establish His kingdom then and there (Lk. 19:11). When He did not fulfill their expectations, they were frustrated and angry enough to kill; but Jesus forgave them (Lk. 23:34). If Jesus could forgive the men who called out "Crucify Him," women, you can forgive men who harbor wrong expectations of you.

Love: Love is patient and kind, and it does not insist on its own way (1 Cor. 13:4-7). Women, you need to remember that all men are different. If you have formed expectations for men that they cannot live up to, it is not their fault. You have the power to change your expectations; and if you find that your expectations of men are unreasonable, you should be flexible.

In everything, women should look to God and trust Him (Prov. 3:5-6). His promises are absolutely sound, and your expectation that He will fulfill His Word is called faith. You can expect God to do exactly what He says He will do (2 Cor. 1:20; Josh. 21:45; Ps. 77:8; 2 Pet. 1:4). When based on God's Word, your expectations will never fail to be met. "The expectation of the Lord is trustworthy" (Ps. 19:7).

Introduction

Here are seven applications to apply on a daily basis to help reduce stereotypical expectations in a woman's life:

I. Find women you can relate to:

One of the most effective ways to overcome stereotypical expectations is to find women who had to overcome similar expectations to the ones you're currently facing.

Build Your Self-Esteem Based on Who You Are as A Person:

When you build your self-esteem around the identities ascribed to your gender, that offers a great avenue and model to follow. In some cases, however, it can limit people to only seeing good in themselves if it reinforces their preconceived notions regarding the relationship between gender and identity.

Network with Others Who Are Promoting Gender Equality.

People in business often do a lot of networking. But in social situations where you're mixing with strangers, it can be easy to stick to groups that are familiar to you. It takes a little effort to break out of your normal sphere.

Move confidently into male-dominated areas and speak up:

Let's be honest: stereotypes won't disappear unless people understand they are harmful. Women in male-dominated environments can help raise awareness. Role models play a crucial role in promoting gender equality and fighting gender stereotypes.

II. Prepare to react:

Women should anticipate and prepare to react to inappropriate or discriminating comments. For example, when the American celebrity Lauren Conrad was asked on radio "What is your favorite position?", she briefly paused and replied "CEO".

Acts 3:5; Jeremiah 33:3

III. Cultivate your thoughts

Another factor that has shown to overcome stereotypical expectations is having a "frame of mind."

Sometimes you have no control as to what thoughts enter your mind; however, you are able to take control of your thoughts. It's important for women to remember that despite outside factors, you still have power and control over the goals you can accomplish in life. And often times by refocusing on your own individual effort, you can improve your cleverness and abilities.

God's Word will help you to recognize your thoughts for what they really are and how to act (or not act) upon them.

Ephesians 4:23; Romans 12:2

IV. Reframe your everyday worries

One of the big reasons stereotypical expectations have such negative influences on women is that they deplete mental resources. Women get so fearful that they are going to fulfill a negative expectation, so they spend more time worrying about that than focusing on the actual expectation at hand.

Philippians 4:6-7

V. Establish yourself and your sense of worth

Having high self-confidence and a sense of self-worth can be important requirements in overcoming stereotypical expectations. Sometimes you can get too caught up in the unconstructive things about yourself that you forget about all the constructive qualities you have.

Reminding yourself of your positive characteristics can help heighten your self-worth and serve you better in minimizing your sensitivity toward stereotypical expectations in the future.

Romans 12:3

VI. Make light of labeling others

Women are complicated people who rarely fit neatly into a single label.

Perhaps you identify strongly as a black woman, but certainly there is much more to your identity than simply your race and gender, right?

In fact, many times there is more diversity within a particular race or gender than there is across different races or gender. One black woman can be a very, different person than another black woman. For example, such as maybe hair choice, mindset toward society, career/work ethic, beliefs toward marriage and children, etc.

We often have many different social identities, but they are part of what make us unique as individuals.

Matthew 7:1-2

VII. Act as if you're your future self

One of the most powerful attitudes to take in your life is to act *as if* you are already your future self.

Often, there's no better way to look beyond society's expectations and overcome stereotypes than to set your own standards on how to live life, how to be seen in the world, how to manage one's career based on your own expectations for yourself in the future.

This can be a huge help because it can often bring you *closer* to thinking and acting in new ways that serve your goals, rather than work against them. When you do this, you're also expanding your sense of identity outside of ways that conform to stereotypes.

You can learn more about this attitude in Jeremiah 29:11.

Chapter 1

INFERIOR TO NONE

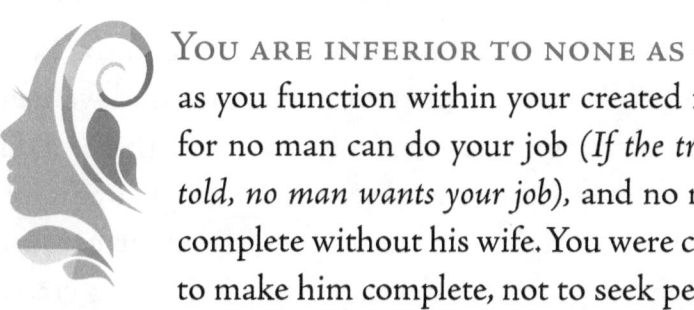

You are inferior to none as long as you function within your created nature, for no man can do your job *(If the truth be told, no man wants your job),* and no man is complete without his wife. You were created to make him complete, not to seek personal fulfillment parallel to him. A woman trying to function like a man is as ridiculous as a man trying to be like a woman. A unisex society is a society dangerously out of order. When you are a helpmeet to your husband, you are a helper to Christ Jesus.

A proper reading of Scripture reveals a high view of women, which is ultimately rooted in creation, and even the controversial passages, when seen in their historical context, agree with this high view. From the very first chapter of Scripture, women are afforded a higher place than in any other ancient writing. In Genesis 1:27, women are said to be created in the image of God just as men are; yet there is a distinction between the two from the beginning.

Application:

That's where we derive human value—not on gender, not on ethnicity, but on the fact every human being is made in the image of God. It says, "Male and female, he created them." (Gen 5: 2). Women, that's where you get your value, not by man's expectations. Now, we do see in the New Testament distinction made between men and women; it's just referring to different roles we have. There's a difference between having a role and having higher or lower value. For example, our values are important because they help us grow and develop. They help us to create the future we want to experience. That's why women must function within their created nature.

In fact, God models this for us. Look at the Trinitarian view of God: Father, Son, and Holy Spirit are all equally God. None is inferior to the other, as they just have different roles that they play. So, it wasn't the Father who died the cross for sins of humanity. It was the Son who willingly submitted His will to the will of the Father. Does that mean the Son was somehow inferior to the Father? Of course not. It was just a difference in role. The Son willingly submitted Himself to the Father, and that is key to women knowing their worth by simply putting their needs and wants before their own. So, when a woman submits to a man, it means to be willing to allow him to lead when there is a disagreement, provided that his leadership is reasonable and just.

Let's look at Ephesians 5 starting at verse 21, which will help women understand a little bit more about this headship and the relationship between husband and wife. It says, "and be subject to one another in the fear of Christ" or to "submit to one another in the fear of Christ." (Eph 5:21)

There's equal value with men and women, but there are different roles that men and women have in marriage relationships. Remember, women—different roles do not equal different value. You are inferior to none.

Chapter 2

GENDER EQUALITY

God Himself elevated the status of women forever when He chose to send His own Son, Jesus Christ, to be born of a virgin. The words and actions of Jesus underscored His elevated opinion of women, as did the early church that was established in His name following His return to heaven:

- His first miracle was performed in response to a plea from His mother (Jn. 2:1-21).

- His first revelation of Himself as Messiah was to a woman (Jn. 4:25-26).

- His greatest miracle was performed at the request of two women (Jn. 11:1-44).

- His death was memorialized by a woman (Jn. 12:1-8).

- Women were included in His expanded group of disciples (Mk. 15:41).

- Women stayed with Him throughout His crucifixion, even after the men had left (Matt. 27:55-56).

- Women observed His burial (Matt. 27:61).

- Following His resurrection, He appeared first to a woman (Jn. 20:1-16).

- He commissioned women as the very first evangelists (Matt. 28:1-10; Jn. 20:17).

The very fact that the Bible goes out of its way to carefully record all of the above reveals the intentionality of God's purpose to reestablish the position of women to that of equality with men. His Son, Jesus Christ, not only bridged the gap between God and man through His death on the cross and made atonement for man's sin, but He removed all barriers including that of gender, race, and nationality.

This was confirmed by the apostle Paul when he stated, "There is neither Jew nor Greek, slave nor free, male nor female, for you are all one in Christ Jesus. If you belong to Christ then you are…heirs according to the promise" (Gal. 3:28-29).

Chapter 3

A WIFE IS THAT GOOD THING

Proverbs 8:22 says, "He who finds a wife finds a good thing and obtain favor the LORD." Wives, you bring favor to your husband, and that's "a good thing."

If you are a wife, you were created to fill a need; and in that capacity, you are a good thing, a helper suited to the needs of a man. This is how God created you, and it is your purpose for existing. You are, by nature, equipped in every way to be your husband's helper.

A good wife makes the home a haven where development and devotion occur. How good it is to have a loyal, faithful, and reliable best friend. A good wife is the teammate who sticks by her husband's side, helps him when he falls, encourages him when he is down, and rejoices when he succeeds.

Applications:

Proverbs 14:1 reveals that a wife will either build or tear down her home. The good wife realize that her primary ministry of her married life is to build her house because she knows her worth and that she is designated as a good thing in the Word of God, but the foolish wife tears her house down with her own hands.

Proverbs 12:4 teaches that having a capable wife is as good as being royalty. "An admirable wife is the crown of her husband, but she who shames him is like rottenness in his bones." Look at the wife's potential—you can be a crown or a tumor to your husband.

Proverbs 18:22 proclaims the blessing that comes from finding a godly wife. "He who finds a wife finds a god thing and obtains favor from the Lord." This favored man sought a wife with care and prayer, and found what he sought. He found the will of God and is prepared for heaven.

Chapter 4

DON'T THINK LIKE MAN

WHEN GOD GAVE EVE TO ADAM, HE was giving a helper, not a conscience. Adam already had a conscience before his wife was created. You are created to be your husband's helper—not his conscience, not his vocational director, and certainly not his critic.

APPLICATIONS:

First Peter 4:1-2 teaches women how to think like Christ. Since Jesus went through everything you're going through and more, learn to think like Him. You are what you think, and you can become what you think!

The Bible is very clearly telling us in the above verse that we can all choose what to think about and dwell on. In other words, we can choose to think about what we want to think about!

Women, you're thinking and thought process do not control you—you control them! For many, this has become an actual, mental stronghold because they have been caught up in this type of depressing thinking for such a long period of time.

You are directly responsible for choosing what you think about and dwell on. Make sure that your thinking always lines up with the Word of God and how He wants you to think about things.

This is one of the main areas the Lord is absolutely going to work on. God wants to decontaminate your thought life and set it straight.

Proverbs 23:7- "For as he thinks in his heart, so is he."

Chapter 5

LIKEWISE, SURRENDER AND HONOR THY HUSBAND

Wives, when you honor your husband, you honor God. When you obey your husband, you obey God. The degree to which you reverence your husband, you reverence your God. The way you will be able to do this is by taking an in-depth look at what submission is, according to 1 Peter 3:1-6

In the same way, you wives, be submissive to your own husbands so that even if any *of them* are disobedient to the word, they may be won without a word by the behavior of their wives, as they observe your chaste and respectful behavior. Your adornment must not be *merely* external—braiding the hair, and wearing gold jewelry, or putting on dresses; but *let it be* the hidden person of the heart, with the imperishable quality of a gentle and quiet spirit, which is precious in the sight of God. For in this way in former times the holy women also, who hoped in God, used to adorn themselves, being submissive to their own husbands; just as Sarah obeyed Abraham, calling him lord, and you have become her children if you do what is right without being frightened by any fear.

Applications:

I. Surrender is not agreeing with everything.

For instance, if your husband is an unbeliever, he doesn't worship the true living God as you do, knowing the almighty God as the song writer "Sinach sings Way Maker; Miracle Worker; Promise Keeper and Light in the Darkness." Do not get divorced over issues of religion, though.

Surrender does not mean you must agree with the opinions of your husbands, even on things as fundamental and serious as the Christian faith.

II. Surrender does not mean you don't have an opinion.

Don't let any man tell you, "I do all the thinking in this family." Now, I am not saying by you having your own thoughts, you don't have to listen to your husband. And don't look for always getting the last word. Sometimes you need to say, "You were right; I was wrong." Women, that statement will go a long way with men…trust me!

III. Surrender does not mean you stop trying to persuade your husband.

Continue to try to persuade your husband. You are a helpmate; you should be devoted in changing him from an unbeliever to a believer. Remember God is the one to change the heart but a wife can be the encouragement to the Christian faith.

IV. Surrender is not putting your husband before Christ.

Don't put the will of your husband before the will of Christ; if you must choose between the two, always choose Jesus.

V. Surrender does not mean relying on your husband for all things spiritual.

Surrender does not mean getting all of your spiritual strength through your husband. Women, your hope is in God.

VI. Surrender does not mean existing or standing in fear.

Surrendering is the calling of a wife to honor and affirm her husband's leadership, and to help carry it by knowing her worth in Christ. Both men and women are called to lead and surrender in marriage.

Chapter 6

WIFE DECEITFUL CHARACTER & WORK

 Eve was totally deceived into thinking that her female intuition, sensitivity, passions, and good looks were spirituality. She had no idea she was a woman in total rebellion against God.

"The serpent said to the woman, 'You surely will not die! For God knows that in the day you eat from it your eyes will be opened, and you will be like God, knowing good and evil'" (Gen. 3:4-5).

Unfortunately, the first account of a woman's actions in the Bible is the one of the most infamous actions in all of Scripture. Eve ate the forbidden fruit and convinced Adam to do the same, resulting in sin and death for themselves and all their descendants. However, nowhere in Scripture is Eve ultimately blamed for the Fall. Uniformly, Adam is blamed for the introduction of death. In this passage, the sentence of death is pronounced to Adam, not Eve (Rom. 5:12-14; 1 Cor. 15:21-22).

A wife who is under Satan's influence will have a character that is deceitful, devious, and cunning in a variety of guises, as he seeks to influence people, through her, for his own ends.

APPLICATIONS:

Satan's deceitful character

He is wicked: Matthew 6:13—"And do not lead us into temptation, but deliver us from evil. For Yours is the kingdom and the power and the glory forever. Amen."

He is deceitful: 2 Corinthians 11:14—"No wonder, for even Satan disguises himself as an angel of light."

He is devious: Ephesians 6:11—"Put on the full armor of God, so that you will be able to stand firm against the schemes of the devil."

He is a slanderer: Job 1:9-11—"Then Satan answered the [a]Lord, 'Does Job fear God for nothing? Have You not made a hedge about him and his house and all that he has, on every side? You have blessed the work of his hands, and his possessions have increased in the land. But put forth Your hand now and touch all that he has; he will surely curse You to Your face.'"

Satan's deceitful work

He deceives folks: 1 Timothy 2:14—"And *it was* not Adam *who* was deceived, but the woman being deceived, fell into transgression."

He works bogus miracles: 2ⁿᵈ Thessalonians 2: 9-10 "*That is*, the one whose coming is in accord with the activity of Satan, with all power and signs and false wonders, and with all the deception of wickedness for those who perish, because they did not receive the love of the truth so as to be saved."

He appoints false prophets: Matthew 7:15— "Beware of the false prophets, who come to you in sheep's clothing, but inwardly are ravenous wolves."

He misuses Scripture: Matthew 4:6—"And *said to Him, 'If You are the Son of God, throw Yourself down;

for it is written, 'He will command His angels concerning You'; and 'On *their* hands they will bear You up, So that You will not strike Your foot against a stone.'"

He blinds unbelievers: 2 Corinthians 4:4—"In whose case the god of this world has blinded the minds of the unbelieving so that they might not see the light of the gospel of the glory of Christ, who is the image of God."

Chapter 7

A WOMAN WHO FEARS THE LORD

Have you ever wanted to be a Proverbs 31 woman? Do you have any idea what it means to be such a woman? Proverbs 31 contains the things a woman must do today if she wants to be a woman who fears the Lord. It doesn't tell a woman what to do to become fearful of the Lord. Rather, this proverb provides a depiction of what flows out of a woman who already fears Him.

Below, you'll find four distinctive qualities of a woman who fears the Lord. They are opportunities to test your heart. If you have the right fear or understanding of God, then these four qualities will overflow in your life.

I. A woman who fears the Lord isn't worried about what's going to happen in her life.

A woman who fears the Lord is not worried about her future, because she knows what Jeremiah 29:11 says: "'For I know the plans that I have for you,' declares the LORD, 'plans for welfare and not for calamity to give you a future and a hope.'" If you have unease, it reveals what you think about God.

II. A woman who fears the Lord speaks knowledge and compassion.

A woman who fears the Lord has useful wisdom. Proverbs 31:26 says, "She opens her mouth in wisdom, and the teaching of kindness is on her tongue." This verse tells a woman that in order to be a good steward of her words, she must know and love God.

III. A woman who fears the Lord is physically powerful.

A woman who fears the Lord is physically powerful. Proverbs 31:17 states, "She girds herself with strength and makes her arms strong." Proverbs 23:17 tells us, "Do not let your heart envy sinners, But *live* in the fear of the LORD always." The woman who continues in the fear of the Lord will have power to defend herself against the envy of what she shouldn't have.

IV. A woman who fears the Lord is for other people, not against them.

A woman who fears the Lord will live not for herself alone but for others. Proverbs 31:11-12 explains, "The heart of her husband trusts in her, and he will have no lack of gain. She does him good and not evil all the days of her life."

Let this list of qualities remind you of the opportunity you have to grow in your fear of the Lord. May this opportunity excite you! Your fear and view of God will play out in your dealings with others. If you believe that God is for you, you can look out for their wellbeing because you know that God is looking out for yours.

This lady believed she could force her husband to submit because she was "spiritually anointed." She did not reckon on God. A woman who thinks she can walk her own way because she believes herself spiritually gifted has no fear of Almighty God.

Chapter 8

THE CHALLENGE RESPONSE: WOMEN KNOW YOUR WORTH

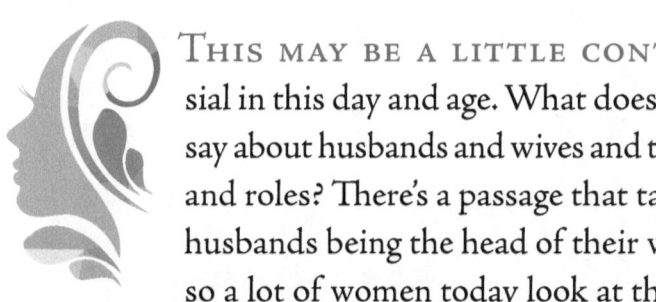

THIS MAY BE A LITTLE CONTROVERSIAL in this day and age. What does the Bible say about husbands and wives and their value and roles? There's a passage that talks about husbands being the head of their wives, and so a lot of women today look at that and go, "What does that mean? Doesn't that mean that men are superior to women?" Well, no, and here is where you need to know your worth. As mentioned earlier, this is just referring to the different roles that we have and does not refer to people having higher or lower value.

There is mutual submission that should happen in a relationship between husband and wife. There's equal value between the two. Husband and wife should be equally valued as they fulfill their different roles.

Christianity dignifies women all throughout Scripture and gives them a whole different status. It's actually Christianity that brings the worth of a woman to the forefront.

Women, be thou helpmeet you were created to be.

All scriptures are from the New American Standard Bible (NASB)

This is my first book of the Beyond Series:

1. Beyond Man's Expectations "Know Your Ture Worth"

2. Beyond Covid 19 "A True Miracle"

3. Beyond "Sunday 4 Walls"

www.ingramcontent.com/pod-product-compliance
Lightning Source LLC
LaVergne TN
LVHW041552060526
838200LV00037B/1250